Y0-CXK-018

EASY FRENCH CULTURE GAMES

Maurie N. Taylor

PASSPORT BOOKS
a division of *NTC Publishing Group*
Lincolnwood, Illinois USA

Introduction

Experience has shown that games and puzzles are among the most effective tools for learning a language. *Easy French Culture Games* contains thirty-nine word games that will not only help you increase your French vocabulary, but will also expand your knowledge of French culture.

The games in this book come in a variety of formats that will challenge and entertain you. The solution for each one will help you learn about French culture. As you solve these puzzles, you will discover French proverbs and literary quotes, as well as learning the names of prominent French authors, painters, and scientists, titles of well-known plays and novels, and many more cultural facts. These puzzles are perfect for advanced beginners, intermediate learners, or even advanced students of French who want to learn more about French culture as they practice their language skills.

You may want to solve these word games on your own or work on them with a friend. However you choose to do them, *Easy French Culture Games* will provide hours of enjoyment. And when you finish each puzzle, you will find an Answer Key at the back of the book to help you check your answers.

1994 Printing

Published by Passport Books, a division of NTC Publishing Group.
©1991 by NTC Publishing Group, 4255 West Touhy Avenue,
Lincolnwood (Chicago), Illinois 60646-1975 U.S.A.
All rights reserved. No part of this book may be reproduced, stored
in a retrieval system, or transmitted in any form or by any means,
electronic, mechanical, photocopying, recording or otherwise, without
the prior permission of NTC Publishing Group.
Manufactured in the United States of America.

3 4 5 6 7 8 9 VP 9 8 7 6 5 4 3 2

Contents

ANAGRAMMES: PROVERBE   Jeu   1

Decide on the French words which answer these English clues
and fill them in letter by letter -- first in the blanks following the definitions, and then in the blanks of the same number
in the diagram below.

ENGLISH CLUES: FRENCH WORDS:

A. "7:15" is sept   Q U A R T
    heures et -----:   14 4 18 12 9

B. First person: J e
                                17 16

C. Purplish color: M A U V E
                                 1 11 8 6 3

D. Second person: T U
                                10 15

E. Two times cinq: D I X
                                13 21 5

F. Late spring month: M A I
                                19 20 2

G. His or her: S E
                                22 7

When you've transferred the right letters into their correct
order below, they will read as a well-known FRENCH
PROVERB:

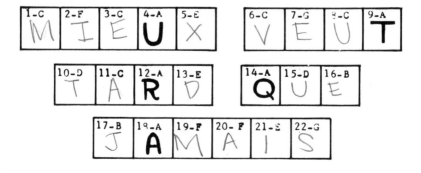

Decide on French words answering the English clues given
and fill them in letter by letter -- first in the blanks following the definitions, and then in the blanks of the same number
in the diagram at the bottom of the page.

ENGLISH CLUES:

A. Head of the family:

$\underline{P}_{22}\ \underline{E}_{4}\ \underline{R}_{3}\ \underline{E}_{16}$

B. Pen, feather:

$\underline{P}_{2}\ \underline{L}_{13}\ \underline{U}_{18}\ \underline{M}_{21}\ \underline{E}_{12}$

C. Half of the French
negative:

$\underline{P}_{8}\ \underline{A}_{17}\ \underline{S}_{23}$

D. Form of the verb
être :

$\underline{E}_{14}\ \underline{S}_{5}$

E. Dairy product:

$\underline{L}_{9}\ \underline{A}_{7}\ \underline{I}_{11}\ \underline{T}_{19}$

F. Form of the verb
avoir:

$\underline{A}_{1}$

G. One color of the
tricolore:

$\underline{B}_{15}\ \underline{L}_{6}\ \underline{E}_{20}\ \underline{U}_{10}$

FRENCH WORDS:

If you've guessed the right words, and transferred the letters
in their correct order, they should spell a FRENCH PROVERB:

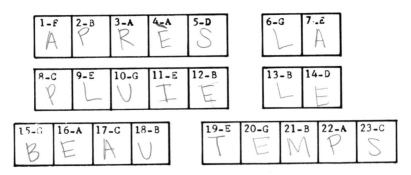

1-F	2-B	3-A	4-A	5-D		6-G	7-..
A	P	R	E	S		L	A

8-C	9-E	10-G	11-E	12-B		13-B	14-D
P	L	U	I	E		L	E

15-G	16-A	17-C	18-B		19-E	20-G	21-B	22-A	23-C
B	E	A	U		T	E	M	P	S

ENGLISH CLUES:	FRENCH WORDS:

A. A basic food; the
    "staff of life":

$$\underset{1}{P}\ \underset{14}{A}\ \underset{19}{I}\ \underset{4}{N}$$

B. Of the, some:

$$\underset{6}{D}\ \underset{11}{E}\ \underset{16}{S}$$

C. Early evening:

$$\underset{13}{S}\ \underset{9}{O}\ \underset{3}{I}\ \underset{8}{R}$$

D. Oldest bridge on the
    Seine is le ---- Neuf:

$$\underset{18}{P}\ \underset{2}{O}\ \underset{20}{N}\ \underset{5}{T}$$

E. It looks "sensible,"
    and means just that:

$$\underset{22}{S}\ \underset{7}{E}\ \underset{15}{N}\ \underset{12}{S}\ \underset{17}{É}$$

F. Himself, herself, or
    themselves (the French
    reflexive pronoun):

$$\underset{10}{S}\ \underset{21}{E}$$

FRENCH PROVERB:

1-A	2-D	3-C	4-A	5-D		6-B	7-E
P	O	I	N	T		D	E

8-C	9-C	10-F	11-B	12-E		13-C	14-A	15-E	16-B
R	O	S	E	S		S	A	N	S

17-E	18-D	19-A	20-D	21-F	22-E
É	P	I	N	E	S

ENGLISH CLUE: FRENCH WORD:

A. More often "child"
    than "infant": $\overline{10}$ $\overline{14}$ $\overline{16}$ $\overline{21}$ $\overline{8}$ $\overline{29}$

B. Hour, or time: $\overline{4}$ $\overline{13}$ $\overline{1}$ $\overline{6}$ $\overline{24}$

C. Room, or hall: $\overline{22}$ $\overline{17}$ $\overline{11}$ $\overline{23}$ $\overline{30}$

D. Part of the leg: $\overline{25}$ $\overline{27}$ $\overline{3}$ $\overline{9}$

E. Mount, as in
    ---- Blanc: $\overline{31}$ $\overline{7}$ $\overline{28}$ $\overline{19}$

F. Filled, full: $\overline{32}$ $\overline{12}$ $\overline{15}$ $\overline{18}$ $\overline{2}$

G. Past participle
    of prendre: $\overline{20}$ $\overline{26}$ $\overline{5}$ $\overline{33}$

FRENCH PROVERB:

1-B	2-F	3-D

4-B	5-G	6-B	7-E	8-A	9-D	10-A	11-C	12-F	13-B

14-A	15-F	16-A	17-C	18-F	19-E	20-G	21-A	22-C

23-C	24-B	25-D	26-G	27-D	28-E	29-A	30-C	31-E	32-F	33-G

ENGLISH CLUES: FRENCH WORDS:

A. Correct, or right:

$\overline{1}$ $\overline{9}$ $\overline{11}$ $\overline{15}$ $\overline{8}$

B. Friends:

$\overline{12}$ $\overline{3}$ $\overline{18}$ $\overline{14}$

C. Half of a dozen:

$\overline{19}$ $\overline{5}$ $\overline{10}$

D. Preposition used
    with entrer:

$\overline{7}$ $\overline{4}$ $\overline{13}$ $\overline{6}$

E. Precious metal:

$\overline{17}$ $\overline{16}$

F. Either "to" or "has,"
    depending on the accent:

$\overline{2}$

FRENCH PROVERB:

1-A	2-F	3-B	4-D	5-C	6-D

7-D	8-A	9-A	10-C		11-A	12-B	13-D	14-B

15-A	16-E	17-E	18-B	19-C

ENGLISH CLUES: FRENCH WORDS:

A. Following, train:

$\overline{18}\ \overline{\ 8}\ \overline{12}\ \overline{\ 1}\ \overline{15}$

B. Cock, rooster:

$\overline{\ 5}\ \overline{\ 2}\ \overline{\ 7}$

C. Brunette color:

$\overline{10}\ \overline{24}\ \overline{\ 3}\ \overline{16}$

D. Post office,
   bureau de -----:

$\overline{20}\ \overline{23}\ \overline{22}\ \overline{\ 4}\ \overline{\ 6}$

E. Masculine article:

$\overline{13}\ \overline{17}$

F. Feminine article:

$\overline{14}\ \overline{21}$

G. Laughs (with il):

$\overline{11}\ \overline{\ 9}\ \overline{19}$

FRENCH PROVERB:

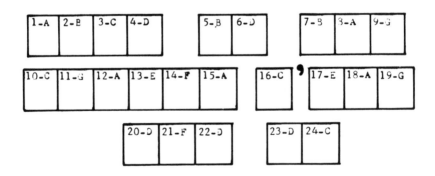

1-A	2-B	3-C	4-D		5-B	6-D		7-B	8-A	9-G

10-C	11-G	12-A	13-E	14-F	15-A		16-C	,	17-E	18-A	19-G

20-D	21-F	22-D		23-D	24-C

ENGLISH CLUES: FRENCH WORDS:

A. Thing:
                                  ‾‾ ‾‾ ‾‾ ‾‾ ‾‾
                                   1 20   8 23   6

B. Leave, depart
    from (with <u>ils</u>):   ‾‾ ‾‾ ‾‾ ‾‾ ‾‾ ‾‾ ‾‾ ‾‾
                                  10 11 15   4   7   2 22 16

C. Wire, thread:
                                  ‾‾ ‾‾ ‾‾
                                  13 12 17

D. Neck, or collar
    (of clothing):   ‾‾ ‾‾ ‾‾
                                  19 24   5

E. Pineapple:
                                  ‾‾ ‾‾ ‾‾ ‾‾ ‾‾ ‾‾
                                  18   9 14 25 21   3

FRENCH PROVERB:

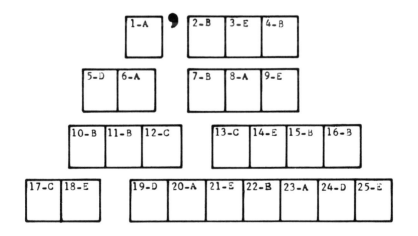

ENGLISH CLUES: FRENCH WORDS:

A. Form of tu:
    ___ ___ ___
     3   24   27

B. Debt, indebtedness:
    ___ ___ ___ ___ ___
    28   2   22   11   16

C. In the manner of
    (two words):   ___   ___ ___
                         6   12   20

D. Paints (with il):
    ___ ___ ___ ___ ___
     1   8   10   25   5

E. Rug, carpet:
    ___ ___ ___ ___ ___
     9   17   7   14   15

F. Times (as in the multi-
    plication table):   ___ ___ ___ ___
                        19   13   21   23

G. United, smooth:
    ___ ___ ___
    18   26   4

FRENCH PROVERB:

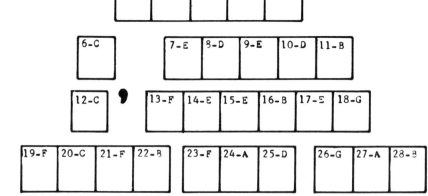

ENGLISH CLUES: FRENCH WORDS:

A. A piece of candy:

$$\overline{18}\ \overline{6}\ \overline{26}\ \overline{11}\ \overline{24}\ \overline{7}$$

B. One hundred:

$$\overline{1}\ \overline{16}\ \overline{14}\ \overline{10}$$

C. Homonym of Word B,
but means "smells":

$$\overline{3}\ \overline{9}\ \overline{21}\ \overline{28}$$

D. Rhymes with Words B
and C; means "slow":

$$\overline{19}\ \overline{27}\ \overline{8}\ \overline{17}$$

E. Bench, or pew:

$$\overline{23}\ \overline{13}\ \overline{25}\ \overline{15}$$

F. Alternate form of
demonstrative <u>ce</u>:

$$\overline{22}\ \overline{2}\ \overline{4}$$

G. Ball (the kind that
Cendrillon attended):

$$\overline{5}\ \overline{20}\ \overline{12}$$

FRENCH PROVERB:

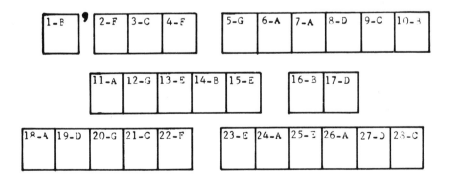

CINQ PEINTRES FRANÇAIS

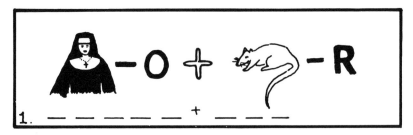

1. _ _ _ _ _ + _ _ _ _

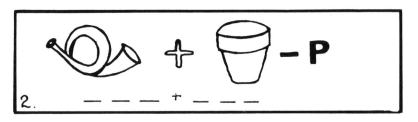

2. _ _ _ _ + _ _ _ _

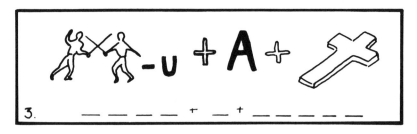

3. _ _ _ _ _ + _ + _ _ _ _ _ _

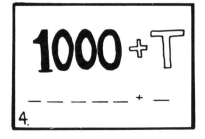

4. _ _ _ _ _ _ + _

5. _ _ + _ _ _ _ _

CINQ COMPOSITEURS FRANÇAIS

1. $\_ \_ \_ \_ \_ + \_ + \_ \_ \_ \_$

2. $\_ \_ \_ \_ \_ \_ \_ + \_ \_ \_ \_$

3. $\_ \_ \_ \_ \_ + \_ \_ \_$

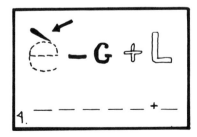

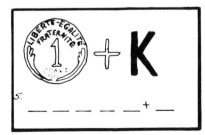

4. $\_ \_ \_ \_ \_ + \_$

5. $\_ \_ \_ \_ \_ \_ + \_$

CINQ PORTS FRANÇAIS

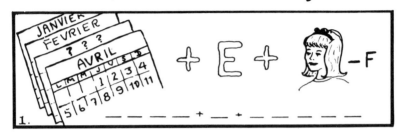

1. _ _ _ _ _ + _ _ + _ _ _ _ _

2. _ _ _ _ _ + _ _ + _ _ _ _ _ + _

3. _ _ _ _   _ _ _ _ _ _ + _ _ _ + _ _ _ _ _

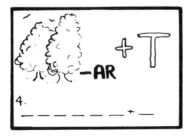

4. _ _ _ _ _ _ + _

5. _ _ _ _ _ + _ _ _ _

CINQ FLEUVES FRANÇAIS

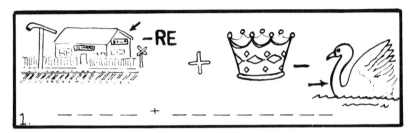

1. _ _ _ _ _ _ + _ _ _ _ _

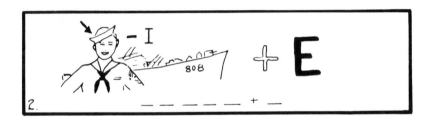

2. _ _ _ _ _ _ + _

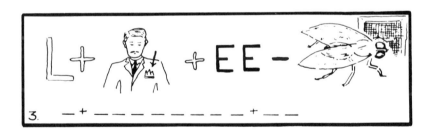

3. _ + _ _ _ _ _ _ _ _ + _ _ _

4. _ _ _ _ _

5. _ _ _ _ _ _ _

CINQ EXPLORATEURS FRANÇAIS

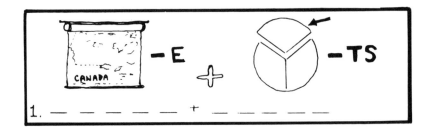

1. _ _ _ _ _ _   +   _ _ _ _ _

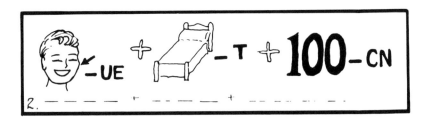

2. _ _ _ _ _ _ _ + _ _ _ _ _ + _ _ _ _ _ _ _

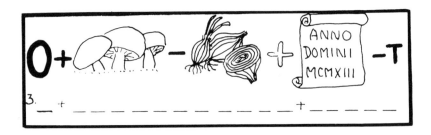

3. _ + _ _ _ _ _ _ _ _ _ _ _ + _ _ _ _

SAMPLE PUZZLE

FRENCH WORDS:	ENGLISH CLUES:
É _ R E _ O N D :	Saint- _____ (Early libertin)
P I S C I N E S :	Swimming pools
É C R A S A N T :	Crushing, overwhelming
S T U P É F I E :	Dumbfounded, stunned
M _ N T _ E U X :	Swiss city
C R A V A T E S :	Neckties
C H A M B R E S :	Bedrooms
C U I L L È R E :	Knife, fork, and --
A G I T E R A S :	Will stir up
C O U S S I N S :	Cushions

AUTEUR:_____   OEUVRE: Les _____

FRENCH WORDS:	ENGLISH CLUES:
P __ I L __ E :	Straw
E __ N U __ S :	Troubles
N __ T I __ E :	Born to (f.)
A __ T I __ E :	Attracts (il)
C __ Û T __ R :	To cost
P __ A I __ E :	Pleads (il)
M __ T T __ Z :	Put --!
A __ F A __ É :	Famished
C __ A Y __ N :	Pencil
F __ R I __ E :	Flour
A __ I M __ L :	Beast
E __ Z É __ A :	Skin disease
D __ M A __ N :	Tomorrow

AUTEUR: _____

ŒUVRE: Le _____

FRENCH WORDS:	ENGLISH CLUES:
O C __ U __ É :	Busy, occupied
F L __ C __ N :	Flake (as snow)
P A __ O __ E :	Speech, word
E N __ U __ É :	Annoyed
A M __ N __ R :	To bring
B R __ E __ X :	French dramatist
P O __ I __ E :	Gendarmes
P E __ O __ E :	Ball (of string)
B R __ V __ T :	Diploma

AUTEUR:_____   OEUVRE:_____

ENGLISH CLUES:	FRENCH WORDS:
To mend, repair:	__ É __ A R E R
Buy, purchase :	__ C __ E T E R
Mangers, cradles:	__ R __ C H E S
Early Americans:	__ N __ I E N S
Sinewy, nervous:	__ E __ V E U X
(For) example:	__ X __ M P L E

AUTEUR:_____   OEUVRE:_____

FRENCH WORDS:		ENGLISH CLUES:
__ U __ É E	:	Rocket (fireworks)
__ I __ N T	:	Winning, charming
__ L __ E R	:	Conjugated with être
__ S __ G E	:	Custom, practice
__ O __ B E	:	Bomb (and iced dessert!)
__ Û __ E S	:	Past tense of avoir (nous)
__ U __ A N	:	Ribbon, band, tape
__ R __ N E	:	Seat of royalty

AUTEUR:_____   OEUVRE:_____

ENGLISH CLUES:		FRENCH WORDS:
Liberté, ___ , Fraternité!	:	__ G __ L I T É
Life work of Debussy	:	__ U __ I Q U E
Signal, badge, insignia	:	__ N __ I G N E
Spotted jungle animal	:	__ É __ P A R D
To take (a person) away	:	__ M __ E N E R
Tempestuous African river	:	__ A __ B È S E
Fragrant, or smelly	:	__ D __ R A N T
Sparetime activities	:	__ O __ S I R S
To come, or to happen	:	__ R __ I V E R

AUTEUR:_____   OEUVRE: 𝓛'_____

FRENCH WORDS:	ENGLISH CLUES:
__ U __ N T :	Hoot, hiss (ils)
__ E __ F S :	Eggs
__ A __ E R :	To swim
__ P __ R A :	Bizet, Gounod, Massenet
__ E __ É E :	Girl's name
__ V __ T E :	Avoids
__ U __ L S :	Encounters à deux
__ N __ I N :	Engine, appliance
__ É __ E T :	French topper
__ M __ N T :	Lover
__ I __ G E :	Linen
__ A __ I G :	Work of Voltaire
__ Ï __ U L :	Grandfather
__ E __ T E :	Feminine demonstrative

AUTEUR: _____

OEUVRE: _____

FRENCH WORDS:	ENGLISH CLUES:
C H __ N __ E U R :	Maurice Chevalier
A I __ E __ O N S :	Airplane parts
G R __ N __ B L E :	French university
D I __ M __ L L E :	Large number (2 wds)
P L __ I __ I R S :	Joys, delights
E N __ E __ I E S :	Very unfriendly women
E N __ R __ I T S :	Places, spots
É P __ O __ V E R :	To test or try
B L __ S __ U R E :	Wound
I N __ I __ U E R :	To show, point out
B O __ Q __ E T S :	Floral arrangements
C O __ M __ N C E :	Begins, starts
F R __ C __ I O N :	Part, portion
D I __ P __ R U E :	Deceased, departed
A P __ L __ Q U É :	Applied, put on
T R __ S __ A R E :	Most unusual (2 wds)
F U __ I __ U S E :	Very angry female
P R __ S __ A N T :	Urgent, imperative

AUTEUR: _____

OEUVRE: *Les* _____

As a final exam in "Literary Ladders," try this one the hard

way, with no clues to help you except the positions of letters

in the French words, and the knowledge that the ladders will

spell vertically, as always, the name of an author and one of

his works -- in this case

A MODERN AUTHOR AND ONE OF HIS EARLY WORKS ---

```
É T __ B __ E
A N __ E __ U
E N __ I __ E
G A __ Ç __ N
P R __ C __ S
J A __ B __ S
P L __ I __ E
F A __ C __ N
M A __ T __ R
F R __ C __ S
U S __ E __ S
S E __ U __ L
```

AUTEUR: _____

OEUVRE: _____

HOW TO SOLVE CHEFS-D' OEUVRE

The "masterpiece" rebuses of this section are solved with the same kind of "word-math" used in MOT-MATH: CINQUES. Note, however, that

1) instead of a series of names or places, CHEFS-D' OEUVRE solve as one continuous rebus spelling out the name of a French book, play, or song;

2) the separation of words in these titles is made easier with comic-strip "balloons" enclosing each word and leading to the next; and

3) separate blanks are provided at the end of each rebus in which to put the title together for final checking.

Always assuming that a children's dancing song that survives for hundreds of years can be styled a "masterpiece" of sorts, notice how this sample CHEF-D' OEUVRE works out, and then try those that follow.

SOLUTION: S U R   L E   P O N T   D'A V I G N O N

UN ROMAN HISTORIQUE DE VICTOR HUGO

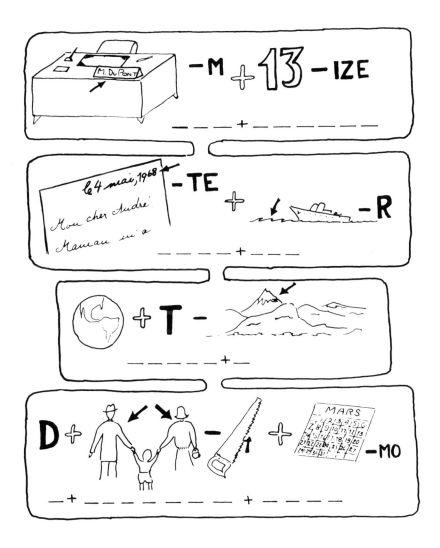

SOLUTION : _ _ _ _ _   _ _ _ _ _ _ _   _ _ _ _ _ _

UNE VIEILLE CHANSON

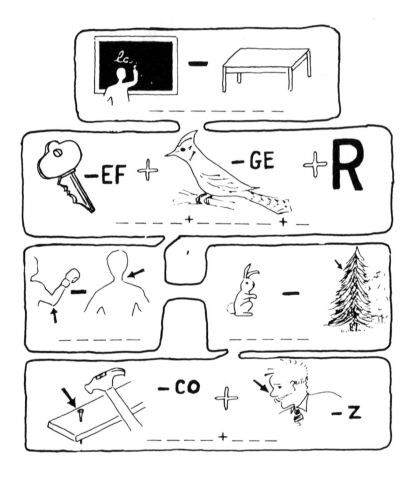

SOLUTION: __ _____ ___ ___ _____

UNE PIÈCE QUI DEVINT UN OPÉRA

SOLUTION: __ _____ __ _____

DEUX CONTES DE DAUDET...

SOLUTION: __ _____ __ ____

SOLUTION: __ _____ _____

...ET UN DE SES ROMANS

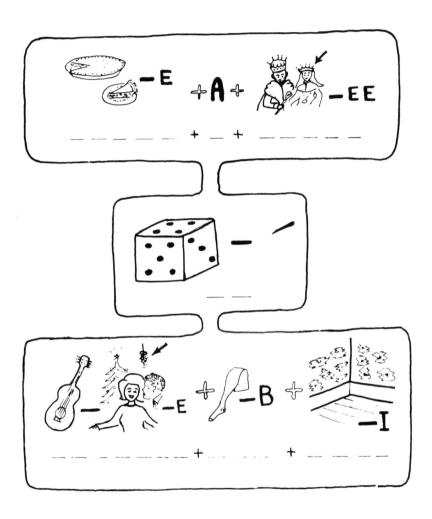

+ _ +

− _ _

+ _ +

Solution: _ _ _ _ _ _ _ _ _ _ _ _ _ _ _ _ _ _

UNE COMÉDIE ET SON AUTEUR

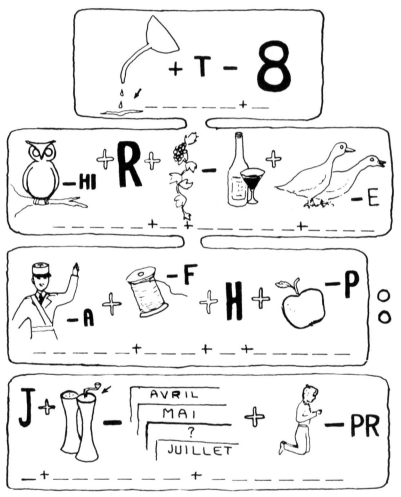

_ _ _ _ _ _ + _ _

SOLUTION: __ _ _ _ _ _ _ _ _ _ _ _ _ _ _

PAR: _ _ _ _ _ _ _ _

TROIS ŒUVRES DE VOLTAIRE

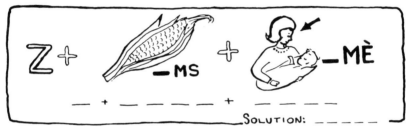

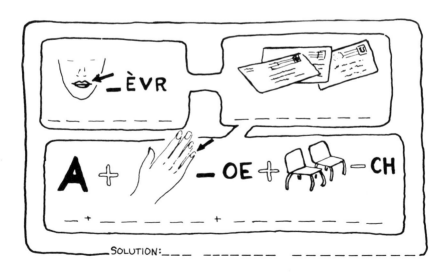

UNE SÉRIE DE ROMANS

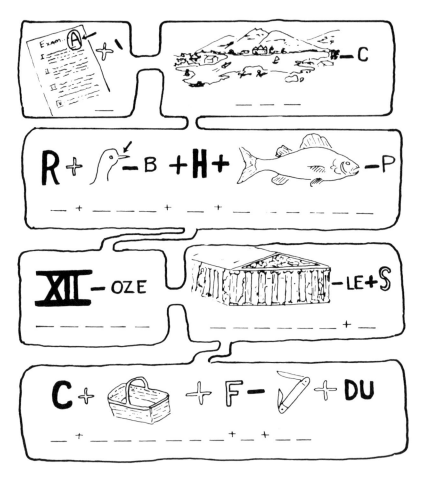

SOLUTION: __ __ __   __ __ __ __ __ __ __ __

__ __   __ __ __ __ __ __   __ __ __ __

ROMANS DE NOS JOURS PAR SAGAN

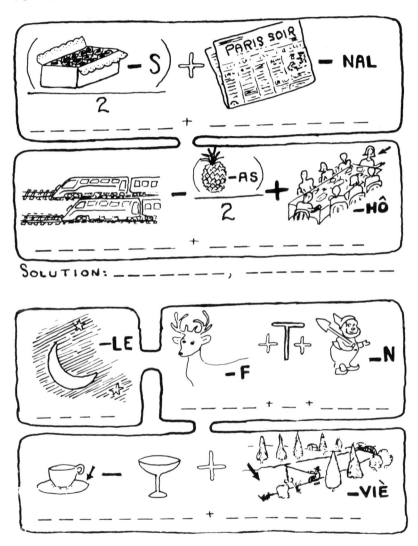

SOLUTION: _ _ _ _ _ _ _ _ , _ _ _ _ _ _ _ _ _ _

SOLUTION: _ _   _ _ _ _ _ _ _   _ _ _ _ _ _ _ _

ANCIENNES PROVINCES DE LA FRANCE

1. X Z E Q Y   (Carrefour de rivières)

   A N J O U
   ─ ─ ─ ─ ─

2. Z Q K A X Z U J W (le 6 juin, 1944)

   ─ ─ ─ ─ ─ ─ ─ ─ ─

3. H K Q B W Z S W (Pays du soleil)

   ─ ─ ─ ─ ─ ─ ─ ─

4. Q K G W X Z X J V   (Pays de Jeanne)

   ─ ─ ─ ─ ─ ─ ─ ─ ─

5. X G V X S W   (Au nord-ouest)

   ─ ─ ─ ─ ─ ─

6. V X B Q J W (Pays des Alpes)

   ─ ─ ─ ─ ─ ─

7. P G X Z U K W (Région industrielle)

   ─ ─ ─ ─ ─ ─ ─

8. O Q Y K X J Z W (Jardin de la France)

   ─ ─ ─ ─ ─ ─ ─ ─

ICI ON PARLE FRANÇAIS --

1. R W Z A J (En Afrique)

   M A R O C
   ‾ ‾ ‾ ‾ ‾

2. R W E W K W X J W Z (Grande île)

   _ _ _ _ _ _ _ _ _

3. J A C K A (Autrefois belge)

   _ _ _ _ _

4. W V K H̃ Z Y H (En Afrique)

   _ _ _ _ _ _ _

5. F B H̃ N H J (Dans l'Amérique du Nord)

   _ _ _ _ _ _

6. N H V K Y F B H (Bruxelles)

   _ _ _ _ _ _ _ _

7. X B Y X X H (Montagnes)

   _ _ _ _ _ _

8. G W Ÿ M Y (Mer des Caraïbes)

   _ _ _ _ _

QUELQUES VEDETTES DE LA FRANCE

1. Y Q J Q X W E M (Chanteuse)

    P A T A C H O U
    ‒ ‒ ‒ ‒ ‒ ‒ ‒

2. Y S Q P (Chanteuse)

    ‒ ‒ ‒ ‒

3. X W Z C Q F S Z B (Chanteur-acteur)

    ‒ ‒ ‒ ‒ ‒ ‒ ‒ ‒ ‒

4. P Z B K Q K G Z F (Acteur comique)

    ‒ ‒ ‒ ‒ ‒ ‒ ‒ ‒ ‒

5. T Q B G E J (Actrice)

    ‒ ‒ ‒ ‒ ‒ ‒

6. V Q T S K (Acteur dramatique)

    ‒ ‒ ‒ ‒ ‒

7. H E K J Q K G (Chanteur-acteur)

    ‒ ‒ ‒ ‒ ‒ ‒ ‒

8. H Q B X Z Q M (Mime)

    ‒ ‒ ‒ ‒ ‒ ‒ ‒

GRANDS POÈTES DE LA FRANCE

1. W V Q Q X K (Bohême)

    <u>V</u> <u>I</u> <u>L</u> <u>L</u> <u>O</u> <u>N</u>

2. Q Z   I X K G Z V K Y (Fabuliste)

    — —   — — — — — — —

3. Q Z F Z J G V K Y (Romantique)

    — — — — — — — —

4. W Y J Q Z V K Y (Symboliste)

    — — — — — — —

5. M J Ý W Y J G (Moderne)

    — — — — — —

6. A Z C U Y Q Z V J Y (Poète français)

    — — — — — — — — —

7. J X K H Z J U (Pléiade)

    — — — — — —

8. P C B X (Au Panthéon)

    — — — —

HOMMES DE SCIENCE DE LA FRANCE

1. H V J E (Médicine)

    R O U X

2. Z J H W K (Physique)

    _ _ _ _ _

3. F Y M B K J H (Bactériologie)

    _ _ _ _ _ _ _

4. P Y C V W M W K H   (Chimie)

    _ _ _ _ _ _ _ _

5. L K Z A J K Ḣ K P (Radioactivité)

    _ _ _ _ _ _ _ _ _

6. F V W T Z Y H Ḱ (Mathématiques)

    _ _ _ _ _ _ _ _

7. Y G F Ḱ H K (Électrodynamiques)

    _ _ _ _ _ _

8. R Y S J K H H K (Photographie)

    _ _ _ _ _ _ _ _

HUIT SCULPTEURS FRANÇAIS

1. X Q Z J   ("La Marseillaise" sur
             l'Arc de Triomphe)

   R U D E

2. X Y Z G V   ("Le Penseur" et
               "Le Baiser")

   _ _ _ _ _

3. K Y Q Z Y V   (Beaucoup de
                 bustes célèbres)

   _ _ _ _ _ _

4. F P X E K Y W Z G   (Statue de la Liberté
                       à New York)

   _ _ _ _ _ _ _ _

5. O P X I J P Q N   (Façade de l'Opéra
                     à Paris)

   _ _ _ _ _ _ _

6. A P G W W Y W   (Connu pour ses statues
                   de femmes)

   _ _ _ _ _ _

7. H G X P X Z Y V   (Style classique de
                     Versailles)

   _ _ _ _ _ _ _

8. O Y Q U E Y Q   (Trois du
                   même nom)

   _ _ _ _ _ _ _

HOW TO DO "ANAGRAMMED QUOTATIONS"

"Anagrammed Quotations" are solved exactly like "Anagrammed Proverbs" (Page 1) except for minor differences in the
diagram (noted at the top of the next page) and the fact that
letters transferred into the diagram spell out a quote from
French prose, poetry, or song, instead of a proverb.

For the "Bonus Clue" help in each of these puzzles, watch the
first letters of the French words on this page. If the words
are correct, their first letters spell vertically the name of
the author, or some other clue to the source of the quotation
being worked out in the diagram.

ANAGRAMMES: CITATION   Jeu   35

Fill in French words
and transfer letters
(by number) into the
diagram opposite:

BONUS CLUE: First letters of
French words below spell the
popular name for the song from
which these lines are taken.
(Add one accent!)

A. Very powerful explosive
    (abbrev.):

$\quad$ T $\quad$ N $\quad$ T
40 $\quad$ 21 $\quad$ 17

B. Dish prepared from
    beaten eggs:

___ ___ ___ ___ ___ ___ ___ ___
27 46 43 44 6 13 50 31

C. Reasoning (present
    participle):

___ ___ ___ ___ ___ ___ ___ ___ ___ ___
32 51 28 1 47 55 16 12 3 30

D. Island of exile for
    Napoleon:

___ ___ ___ ___
33 25 11 54

E. A kind of bridge the
    Romans built:

___ ___ ___ ___ ___ ___ ___
35 18 48 39 56 42 8

F. Dramatist, or play-
    wright:

___ ___ ___ ___ ___ ___ ___ ___ ___ ___
37 49 15 10 45 52 19 36 4 23

G. A kind of soup Parisians
    like:

___ ___ ___ ___ ___ ___
2 24 34 7 22 26

H. A vehicle used in
    space programs:

___ ___ ___ ___ ___ ___ ___ ___
29 9 41 20 5 14 53 38

When letters from the French words on the preceding page are transferred in numerical order into the diagram below, they will read--left to right, line by line--as a French quote.

Black squares, wherever they occur, indicate the beginning of a new word. Square 32-C, for example, will be the first letter of a 7-letter word continued on the next line.

Unfinished words in the diagram can sometimes give helpful leads back to the French key words on the preceding page.

	1-C	2-G	3-C	4-F	5-H		6-B	7-G	
8-E	9-H	10-F	11-D	12-C	13-B	14-H	15-F	16-C	17-A T
	18-E	19-F ,	20-H	21-A N		22-G	23-F	24-G	25-D
	26-G	27-B	28-C	29-H		30-C	31-B		32-C
33-D	34-G	35-E	36-F	37-F	38-H		39-E	40-A T	
41-H	42-E	43-B		44-B ,	45-F	46-B	47-C	48-E	49-F
	50-B ,	51-C	52-F	53-H	54-D	55-C	56-E		

NAME OF THIS SONG: _____

(Answer from "Bonus Clue" filled in here--spelled vertically by first letters of the French words on the preceding page.)

BONUS CLUE: First letters of
the French words below spell
vertically the author of the
quotation on the opposite page.

ENGLISH CLUES: FRENCH WORDS:

A. Who, whom, which:

$\overline{17}$ $\overline{5}$ $\overline{9}$ $\overline{14}$ $\overline{51}$ $\overline{45}$

B. Appetite, desire:

$\overline{27}$ $\overline{2}$ $\overline{31}$ $\overline{30}$ $\overline{12}$ $\overline{25}$ $\overline{19}$

C. Flees, flies (il):

$\overline{16}$ $\overline{28}$ $\overline{44}$ $\overline{50}$

D. Open! (Imperative):

$\overline{13}$ $\overline{43}$ $\overline{24}$ $\overline{23}$ $\overline{21}$ $\overline{8}$

E. Our continent, Amé-
   rique du ----: $\overline{33}$ $\overline{48}$ $\overline{4}$ $\overline{35}$

F. Ballet skirt:

$\overline{26}$ $\overline{22}$ $\overline{20}$ $\overline{40}$

G. Accepts (il):

$\overline{1}$ $\overline{37}$ $\overline{47}$ $\overline{7}$ $\overline{3}$ $\overline{15}$ $\overline{32}$

H. Ideal:

$\overline{41}$ $\overline{29}$ $\overline{46}$ $\overline{18}$ $\overline{39}$

I. Only (with verb):

$\overline{6}$ $\overline{38}$ $\overline{42}$ $\overline{10}$ $\overline{36}$

J. Form of avoir (je):

$\overline{11}$ $\overline{49}$ $\overline{34}$

When letters from the French words on the preceding page are transferred in numerical order into the diagram below, they will read--left to right, line by line--as a French quote.

Black squares indicate the beginning of each new word.

1-G	2-B	3-G	4-E	5-A	6-I	7-G	8-D	
9-A	10-I	11-J		12-B	13-D	14-A	15-G	
16-C	17-A	18-H	19-B	20-F	21-D	22-F	23-D	
24-D	25-B	26-F		27-B	28-C		29-H	30-B
31-B	32-G	33-E	34-J		35-E	36-I		37-G
38-I	39-H	40-F	41-H		42-I	43-D	44-C	
	45-A	46-H	47-G	48-E	49-J	50-C	51-A	

AUTHOR OF THESE LINES:_____

(From "Bonus Clue.")

BONUS CLUE: First letters
of the French words below
spell vertically the author of
the quotation on the opposite
page.

ENGLISH CLUES: FRENCH WORDS:

A. Really, truly:
                              $\overline{67}\ \overline{23}\ \overline{49}\ \overline{60}\ \overline{65}\ \overline{3}\ \overline{27}\ \overline{31}$

B. Houses, buildings
   (immovables!): $\overline{18}\ \overline{64}\ \overline{11}\ \overline{35}\ \overline{46}\ \overline{73}\ \overline{74}\ \overline{8}\ \overline{13}$

C. Flirts (Noun):
                              $\overline{24}\ \overline{68}\ \overline{1}\ \overline{72}\ \overline{5}\ \overline{34}\ \overline{55}\ \overline{10}\ \overline{40}$

D. To touch, concern:
                              $\overline{19}\ \overline{21}\ \overline{69}\ \overline{37}\ \overline{25}\ \overline{66}\ \overline{58}$

E. Offensive:
                              $\overline{71}\ \overline{51}\ \overline{16}\ \overline{41}\ \overline{43}\ \overline{36}\ \overline{75}\ \overline{17}$

F. Relation, or connection:
                              $\overline{30}\ \overline{44}\ \overline{20}\ \overline{4}\ \overline{32}\ \overline{52}\ \overline{45}$

G. French sculpteur:
                              $\overline{38}\ \overline{53}\ \overline{2}\ \overline{7}\ \overline{63}\ \overline{61}$

H. Seizes, usurps:
                              $\overline{6}\ \overline{14}\ \overline{50}\ \overline{47}\ \overline{12}\ \overline{48}$

I. Gaseous (f. pl.):
                              $\overline{28}\ \overline{26}\ \overline{77}\ \overline{76}\ \overline{33}\ \overline{70}\ \overline{59}\ \overline{56}$

J. Oily, unctuous (f.):
                              $\overline{39}\ \overline{54}\ \overline{62}\ \overline{9}\ \overline{22}\ \overline{57}\ \overline{15}\ \overline{42}\ \overline{29}$

When letters from the French words on the preceding page
are transferred in numerical order into the diagram below,
they will read--left to right, line by line--as a French quote.

Black spaces indicate the beginning of each new word.

1-C	2-G	3-A		4-F	5-C	6-H		7-G	8-B	
9-J	10-C	11-B	12-H	13-B		14-H	15-J	16-E	17-E	18-B
19-D		20-F	21-D	22-J	23-A		24-C	25-D	26-I	27-A
28-I	29-J	30-F		31-A	32-F	33-I	34-C	35-B	36-E	
37-D	38-G	39-J	40-C	41-E	42-J		43-E	44-F	45-F	46-B
47-H	48-H		49-A	50-H		51-E	52-F	53-G	54-J	55-C
	56-I	57-J	58-D	59-I	60-A	61-G		62-J	63-G	64-B
65-A	66-D		67-A	68-C	69-D	70-I		71-E	72-C	73-B
			74-B	75-E	76-I	77-I				

AUTHOR OF THESE LINES: _____

(From "Bonus Clue.")

BONUS CLUE: First letters
of the French words below
spell vertically the author of
the quotation on the opposite
page.

ENGLISH CLUES: FRENCH WORDS:

A. More than (2 words):
$\overline{28}\ \overline{4}\ \overline{44}\ \overline{50}\quad \overline{65}\ \overline{61}\ \overline{5}$

B. Match (to strike):
$\overline{37}\ \overline{41}\ \overline{57}\ \overline{6}\ \overline{13}\ \overline{18}\ \overline{54}\ \overline{72}\ \overline{8}$

C. Only, sole:
$\overline{19}\ \overline{11}\ \overline{39}\ \overline{43}\ \overline{63}\ \overline{45}$

D. Lamp, light:
$\overline{47}\ \overline{10}\ \overline{24}\ \overline{3}\ \overline{30}$

E. Thieves, robbers:
$\overline{38}\ \overline{79}\ \overline{27}\ \overline{62}\ \overline{81}\ \overline{20}\ \overline{33}$

F. Yet, still:
$\overline{42}\ \overline{77}\ \overline{78}\ \overline{14}\ \overline{82}\ \overline{49}$

G. Regulation, rule:
$\overline{35}\ \overline{71}\ \overline{60}\ \overline{36}\ \overline{25}\ \overline{23}\ \overline{56}\ \overline{15}\ \overline{32}$

H. Gleam, glimmer:
$\overline{2}\ \overline{66}\ \overline{80}\ \overline{34}\ \overline{7}$

I. Accomplished:
$\overline{58}\ \overline{16}\ \overline{21}\ \overline{17}\ \overline{75}\ \overline{68}\ \overline{40}\ \overline{1}$

J. Illustrated (f.):
$\overline{26}\ \overline{46}\ \overline{29}\ \overline{31}\ \overline{12}\ \overline{55}\ \overline{73}\ \overline{69}\ \overline{48}$

K. Wedding:
$\overline{59}\ \overline{76}\ \overline{52}\ \overline{74}$

L. Spot, place:
$\overline{53}\ \overline{70}\ \overline{9}\ \overline{64}\ \overline{22}\ \overline{67}\ \overline{51}$

When letters from the French words on the preceding page are transferred in numerical order into the diagram below, they will read--left to right, line by line--as a French quote.

Black spaces indicate the beginning of each new word.

1-I	2-H		3-D	4-A	5-A	6-B	7-H	8-B	
9-L	10-D	11-C	12-J		13-B	14-F	15-G		16-I
17-I	18-B	19-C	20-E		21-I	22-L	23-G	24-D	25-G
	26-J	27-E		28-A	29-J	30-D	31-J	32-G	
33-E	34-H	35-G		36-G	37-B		38-E	39-C	40-I
41-B	42-F		43-C	44-A	45-C	46-J	47-D	48-J	
49-F	50-A	51-L		52-K	53-L	54-B	55-J	56-G	
57-B	58-I	59-K	60-G	61-A	62-E	63-C	64-L		65-A
66-H	67-L		68-I	69-J	70-L	71-G	72-B	73-J	74-K
	75-I	76-K	77-F		78-F	79-E	80-H	81-E	82-F

AUTHOR: _____

(From "Bonus Clue.")

BONUS CLUE: First letters
of the French words below
spell vertically the origin of
the quotation on the opposite
page.

ENGLISH CLUES: FRENCH WORDS:

A. Laminate, roll:

$\overline{13}$ $\overline{1}$ $\overline{73}$ $\overline{59}$ $\overline{89}$ $\overline{33}$ $\overline{40}$

B. Aware, up-to-date
   (two words):
$\overline{7}$ $\overline{92}$ $\overline{21}$ $\overline{72}$ $\overline{25}$ $\overline{55}$ $\overline{16}$ $\overline{45}$ $\overline{31}$

C. Handkerchiefs:

$\overline{2}$ $\overline{22}$ $\overline{48}$ $\overline{81}$ $\overline{66}$ $\overline{37}$ $\overline{19}$ $\overline{62}$ $\overline{77}$

D. Abbot, priest:

$\overline{41}$ $\overline{74}$ $\overline{60}$ $\overline{57}$

E. Draftsmen, writers:

$\overline{5}$ $\overline{64}$ $\overline{24}$ $\overline{75}$ $\overline{8}$ $\overline{82}$ $\overline{54}$ $\overline{30}$ $\overline{18}$ $\overline{90}$

F. Succeeded (participial
   form):
$\overline{50}$ $\overline{4}$ $\overline{71}$ $\overline{65}$ $\overline{86}$ $\overline{11}$ $\overline{67}$

G. Hell, hades:

$\overline{20}$ $\overline{23}$ $\overline{87}$ $\overline{44}$ $\overline{93}$

H. Intoxication:

$\overline{32}$ $\overline{79}$ $\overline{9}$ $\overline{70}$ $\overline{94}$ $\overline{35}$ $\overline{12}$

I. Wash house:

$\overline{51}$ $\overline{78}$ $\overline{43}$ $\overline{3}$ $\overline{26}$ $\overline{68}$

J. Long (mas., pl..):

$\overline{58}$ $\overline{29}$ $\overline{34}$ $\overline{46}$ $\overline{38}$

K. Feminine, plural of
   Word D above:
$\overline{14}$ $\overline{53}$ $\overline{39}$ $\overline{91}$ $\overline{27}$ $\overline{84}$ $\overline{47}$ $\overline{6}$

L. Identity:

$\overline{52}$ $\overline{85}$ $\overline{83}$ $\overline{36}$ $\overline{76}$ $\overline{69}$ $\overline{17}$ $\overline{10}$

M. Number of days in an
   American week:
$\overline{42}$ $\overline{80}$ $\overline{15}$ $\overline{56}$

N. To sue, bring action
   (legal term):
$\overline{61}$ $\overline{28}$ $\overline{63}$ $\overline{88}$ $\overline{49}$

When letters from the French words on the preceding page are transferred in numerical order into the diagram below, they will read--left to right, line by line--as a French quote.

Black squares indicate the beginning of each new word.

1-A	2-C	3-I	4-F	5-E		6-K	7-B	8-E	9-H	10-L
	11-F	12-H		13-A	14-K		15-M	16-B	17-L	18-E
19-C	20-G		21-B	22-C	23-G	24-E	25-B	26-I	27-K	
28-N	29-J	30-E	31-B	32-H	33-A	34-J	35-H		36-L	37-C
38-J		39-K	40-A	41-D	42-M		43-I	44-G	45-B	46-J
47-K	48-C	49-N	50-F		51-I	52-L	53-K	54-E	55-B	56-M
57-D		58-J	59-A	60-D	61-N	62-C	63-N	64-E		65-F
66-C	67-F	68-I	69-L	70-H		71-F	72-B	73-A	74-D	75-E
76-L	77-C		78-I	79-H	80-M	81-C		82-E	83-L	84-K
	85-L	86-F	87-G	88-N	89-A	90-E	91-K	92-B	93-G	94-H

NAME OF THIS SONG:_____

(From "Bonus Clue.")

Answer Key

Anagrammed Proverb — Game 1
A. quart; B. je; C. mauve; D. tu; E. dix; F. mai; G. sa
Proverb: Mieux vaut tard que jamais.

Anagrammed Proverb — Game 2
A. père; B. plume; C. pas; D. es; E. lait; F. a; G. bleu
Proverb: Après la pluie, le beau temps.

Anagrammed Proverb — Game 3
A. pain; B. des; C. soir; D. pont; E. sensé; F. se
Proverb: Point de roses sans épines.

Anagrammed Proverb — Game 4
A. enfant; B. heure; C. salle; D. pied; E. mont; F. plein; G. pris
Proverb: Une hirondelle ne fait pas le printemps.

Anagrammed Proverb — Game 5
A. juste; B. amis; C. six; D. dans; E. or; F. a
Proverb: Jamais deux sans trois.

Anagrammed Proverb — Game 6
A. suite; B. coq; C. brun; D. poste; E. le; F. la; G. rit
Proverb: Tout ce qui brille n'est pas or.

Anagrammed Proverb — Game 7
A. chose; B. quittent; C. fil; D. col; E. ananas
Proverb: C'est le ton qui fait la chanson.

Anagrammed Proverb — Game 8
A. toi; B. dette; C. à la; D. peint; E. tapis; F. fois; G. uni
Proverb: Petit à petit, l'oiseau fait son nid.

Anagrammed Proverb — Game 9
A. bonbon; B. cent; C. sent; D. lent; E. banc; F. cet; G. bal
Proverb: C'est bonnet blanc et blanc bonnet.

Word-Math Fives — Game 10
Five French painters:
1. S(o)EUR + (r)AT = SEURAT
2. COR + (p)OT = COROT
3. D(u)EL + A + CROIX = DELACROIX
4. MILLE + T = MILLET
5. RE + NOIR = RENOIR

Word-Math Fives — Game 11
Five French composers:
1. B(a)l(n) + Z + (n)ET = BIZET
2. GOU(tte) + NO(r)D = GOUNOD
3. DEB(o)U(t) + SSY = DEBUSSY
4. (g)RAVE + L = RAVEL
5. FRANC + K = FRANCK

Word-Math Fives — Game 12
Five French ports:
1. MARS + E + (f)ILLE = MARSEILLE
2. CHE(f) + RB + OUR(s) + G = CHERBOURG
3. (i)LE + (c)HA(ise) + (aux) + (li)VRE = LE HAVRE
4. (ar)BRES + T = BREST
5. BORD + EAUX = BORDEAUX

Word-Math Fives — Game 13
Five French rivers:
1. GA(re) + (cou)RONNE = GARONNE
2. MAR(i)N + E = MARNE
3. L + (mouch)OIR + (e)E = LOIRE
4. SOMME (sum of the addition)
5. SEINE (seining net)

Word-Math Fives — Game 14
Five French explorers:
1. CART(e) + (t)IER(s) = CARTIER
2. JO(ue) + LI(t) + (c)E(n)T = JOLIET
3. (o) + CHAMP(ignons) + LA(t)IN = CHAMPLAIN
4. LA SALLE (hall, classroom)
5. MARQUE + TTE = MARQUETTE

Literary Ladders — Game 15
PAILLE
ENNUIS

NATIVE
ATTIRE
COÛTER
PLAIDE
METTEZ
AFFAMÉ
CRAYON
FARINE
ANIMAL
ECZÉMA
DEMAIN
Author: Anatole France
Work: *Le Livre de Mon Ami*

Literary Ladders   **Game 16**

OCCUPÉ
FLOCON
PAROLE
ENNUYÉ
AMENER
BRIEUX
POLICE
PELOTE
BREVET
Author: Corneille
Work: *Polyeucte*
RÉPARER
ACHETER
CRÈCHES
INDIENS
NERVEUX
EXEMPLE
Author: Racine
Work: *Phèdre*

Literary Ladders   **Game 17**

FUSÉE
LIANT
ALLER
USAGE
BOMBE
EUMES
RUBAN
TRÔNE
Author: Flaubert
Work: *Salammbô*
ÉGALITÉ
MUSIQUE
INSIGNE
LÉOPARD
EMMENER

ZAMBÈSE
ODORANT
LOISIRS
ARRIVER
Author: Emile Zola
Work: *L'Assommoir*

Literary Ladders   **Game 18**

HUENT
OEUFS
NAGER
OPÉRA
RENÉE
ÉVITE
DUELS
ENGIN
BÉRET
AMANT
LINGE
ZADIG
AÏEUL
CETTE
Author: Honoré de Balzac
Work: *Eugénie Grandet*

Literary Ladders   **Game 19**

CHANTEUR
AILERONS
GRENOBLE
DIXMILLE
PLAISIRS
ENNEMIES
ENDROITS
ÉPROUVER
BLESSURE
INDIQUER
BOUQUETS
COMMENCE
FRACTION
DISPARUE
APPLIQUÉ
TRÈSRARE
FURIEUSE
PRESSANT
Author: Alexandre Dumas Père
Work: *Les Trois Mousquetaires*

Literary Ladders   **Game 20**

ÉTABLE
ANNEAU
ENDIVE

GARÇON
PRÉCIS
JAMBES
PLAIRE
FALCON
MARTYR
FRACAS
USUELS
SEXUEL
Author: André Malraux
Work: *La Voie Royale*

Masterpiece   Game 21
Historic novel by Victor Hugo:
NO(m) + TRE(ize) = NOTRE
DA(te) + ME(r) = DAME
(mon)DE + (t)–(mont) = DE
(d) + PAR(ents) + (mo)IS = PARIS

Masterpiece   Game 22
An old song:
(table)AU = AU
CL(ef) + (ge)AI + R = CLAIR
(cou)DE = DE
LA(pin) = LA
(c)L(o)U + NE(z) = LUNE

Masterpiece   Game 23
A play that became an opera:
(bal)LE = LE
BARB(e) + (h)IER = BARBIER
DE(ux) = DE
SE(pt) + accent + VILLE = SÉVILLE
Note: Play by Beaumarchais
      Opera by Rossini

Masterpiece   Game 24
Two of Daudet's tales:
LA(it) = LA
M(o)UL(in) + E = MULE
(p) + D(o)U(che) = DU
PAP(i)E(r) = PAPE
(p)LA(t) = LA
"Last" girl = DERNIERE
C(o)L + (t)ASSE = CLASSE
. . . and one of his novels:
TART(e) + A + R(e)IN(e) = TARTARIN
DÉ (minus accent) = DE
(gui)TAR(e) + (b)AS + CO(i)N = TARASCON

Masterpiece   Game 25
A comedy and its author:
(hui)LE + (t) = LE
(hi)BOU + R + (vi)G(n)E + OI(e)S = BOURGEOIS
(a)GENT + (f)IL + H + (p)OMME =
    GENTILHOMME
(j) + MO(u)L(in) + (pr)IÈRE = MOLIÈRE

Masterpiece   Game 26
Three of Voltaire's works:
C(h)AND(elle) + ID(é)E = CANDIDE
Z + (m)AÏ(s) + (mè)RE = ZAÏRE
L(èvr)ES = LES
Lettres = LETTRES
A + (o)NGL(e) + (ch)AISES = ANGLAISES
(or *Lettres Philosophiques*)

Masterpiece   Game 27
A series of novels:
A + accent = À
LA(c) = LA
R + (b)EC + H + (p)ERCHE = RECHERCHE
D(o)U(ze) = DU
TEMP(le) + S = TEMPS
(c) + P(ani)ER + (f) = PERDU
Note: Series by Marcel Proust

Masterpiece   Game 28
Modern novels by Sagan:
BONBON(s) ÷ 2 = BON + JOUR(nal) =
    BONJOUR
TR(a)I(n)S + (hô)TESSE = TRISTESSE
(l)UN(e) = UN
CER(f) + T + (n)AIN = CERTAIN
SOU(coupe) + RI(viè)RE = SOURIRE

Cryptographs   Game 29
Old provinces of France:
1. Anjou; 2. Normandie; 3. Provence;
    4. Orléanais; 5. Alsace; 6. Savoie; 7. Flandre;
8. Touraine

Cryptographs   Game 30
French spoken here—
1. Maroc; 2. Madagascar; 3. Congo; 4. Algérie;
    5. Québec; 6. Belgique; 7. Suisse; 7. Haïti

Cryptographs   Game 31
Some stars from France:

1. Patachou; 2. Piaf; 3. Chevalier; 4. Fernandel;
   5. Bardot; 6. Gabin; 7. Montand; 8. Marceau

Cryptographs   Game 32
Great poets of France:
1. Villon; 2. La Fontaine; 3. Lamartine;
   4. Verlaine; 5. Prévert; 6. Baudelaire;
   7. Ronsard; 8. Hugo

Cryptographs   Game 33
Scientists of France:
1. Roux; 2. Curie; 3. Pasteur; 4. Lavoisier;
   5. Becquerel; 6. Poincaré; 7. Ampère;
   8. Daguerre

Cryptographs   Game 34
Eight French sculptors:
1. Rude; 2. Rodin; 3. Houdon; 4. Bartholdi;
   5. Carpeaux; 6. Maillol; 7. Girardon;
   8. Coustou

Anagrammed Quote   Game 35
A. TNT; B. omelette; C. raisonnant; D. Elbe;
   E. aqueduc; F. dramaturge; G. oignon;
   H. roquette

Quotation: Songe en combattant qu'un oeil
   noir te regarde, et que l'amour t'attend...
Name of the song: "Toreador song" from
   Bizet's *Carmen*

Anagrammed Quote   Game 36
A. lequel; B. appétit; C. fuit; D. ouvrez; E. nord;
   F. tutu; G. accepte; H. idéal; I. ne...que;
   J. eus

Quotation: Apprenez que tout flatteur vit au
   dépens de celui qui l'écoute...
Author: La Fontaine (from *Le Corbeau et Le
   Renard*)

Anagrammed Quote   Game 37
A. vraiment; B. immeubles; C. coquettes;
   D. toucher; E. offensif; F. rapport; G. Houdon;
   H. usurpe; I. gazeuses; J. onctueuse

Quotation: Que peu de temps suffit pour
   changer toutes choses. Nature au front
   serein, comme vous oubliez!
Author: Victor Hugo (from *Tristesse d'Olympio*)

Anagrammed Quote   Game 38
A. plus que; B. allumette; C. unique; D. lampe;
   E. voleurs; F. encore; G. règlement; H. lueur;
   I. accompli; J. illustrée; K. noce; L. endroit

Quotation: Il pleure dans mon coeur comme il
   pleut sur la ville. Quelle est cette langeur qui
   pénètre mon coeur?
Author: Paul Verlaine

Anagrammed Quote   Game 39
A. laminer; B. au courant; C. mouchoirs;
   D. abbé; E. rédacteurs; F. succédé; G. enfer;
   H. ivresse; I. lavoir; J. longs; K. abbesses;
   L. identité; M. sept; N. ester

Quotation: Amour sacré de la patrie, conduis,
   soutiens nos bras vengeurs. Liberté, liberté
   chérie, combats avec tes défenseurs...*(La
   Marseillaise)*

NTC PUZZLE AND LANGUAGE GAME BOOKS

Multilingual Resources
Puzzles & Games in Language Teaching

Spanish
Easy Spanish Word Power Games
Classroom Games in Spanish
Spanish Crossword Puzzles
Spanish Verbs and Vocabulary Bingo Games
Spanish Culture Puzzles
Spanish Vocabulary Puzzles
Let's Play Games in Spanish, 1, 2

French
Jouez le jeu!
Let's Play Games in French
Classroom Games in French
French Crossword Puzzles
French Word Games
French Grammar Puzzles
French Verbs and Vocabulary Bingo Games
French Word Games for Beginners
French Culture Puzzles

German
German Crossword Puzzles
German Word Games for Beginners
Let's Play Games in German

Italian
Italian Crossword Puzzles

Japanese
Let's Play Games in Japanese

Chinese
Let's Play Games in Chinese

For further information or a current catalog, write:
National Textbook Company
a division of *NTC Publishing Group*
4255 West Touhy Avenue
Lincolnwood, Illinois 60646-1975 U.S.A.